# ANTHEM FOR PACIFIC AVENUE

*poems by*

Jeff Alfier

*"Your heart sometimes neglects its proper song."*

*— Baudelaire*

## *Acknowledgments*

Grateful acknowledgments are made to the following publications in which these poems first appeared, sometimes in slightly different forms:

*The Binnacle*
LA Redux on an Ancient Parable
*Border Crossing*
Anthem for Pacific Avenue
*Chiron Review*
Redondo Beach Notebook; Taking on the Record LA Heat
*Concho River Review*
Two Urchin Divers at Terminal Island
*Connecticut River Review*
Thursday at the Torrance Salvation Army Thrift Shop
*Cutthroat*
San Pedro Harbor, Where the Music Lay
*East Coast Literary Review*
Shipyard Sonata; Syllabic Lines for Laundry Hung Dirty on a Friday Afternoon
*Free State Review*
The Week after Mass at Saint Alphonsus, East LA
*Gargoyle*
Stopping at Texas Looseys on a Warm Monday Homeward
*Hurricane Review*
Terminal Island, Los Angeles Harbor
*I-70 Review*
After Losing the Plea Bargain
*Jelly Bucket*
House at the Corner of Live Oak and Wheeler Canyon
*Illuminations*
This Far North of Mojave
*Kentucky Review*
Artesia Boulevard Story
*Lummox*
Travel Music

# Contents

*For those I've lost along the way.*

# *Motel Beyond Beacon Station, California*

She phoned the front desk that morning.
Needed a second night — some vague

imperative to stay put. But our rooms
were booked long before she hit town.

I'd made her vacate. I paused at the door
she didn't close. Absently scanned

the room. Cigarette
stains on the night stand.

Shell Station cup filled
with butts. Half-eaten burrito

flattened beside the phone. The maid
pushed past me. I headed back

to my office. Day's first light
stood in the lobby.

# Torrance Urban Image: Morning Walk

The junk collector's truck speeds past.
Rails of a brass bed arbored upward

in its trailer, their sheen diminished
in light ebbed by maritime fog.

Standing in a driveway in checkered
blue pajamas, an old man with mussed

hair sees his wife off.
She opens the car door. The sound

of their kiss sinks in the rasp
of magnolia leaves. I pass a dead

crow on the neighbor's lawn. This time,
the blue-black sheen of wings

gathered close against its body, head
bowed — almost regal, compelled to fall.

# *Your Side of Odessa Canyon*

All distance is biblical. Your life
an encampment in the wilderness
of Exodus, a reed shaken in the wind.


The snake you didn't crush beds down
beneath dying oleanders. Your barn,
disused for a decade, leans south,


shoulders-back a hard wind
that tells you nothing you do not know.
It lifts torn screens like a voyeur.


Few neighbors now. The Jenny Rose
diner, down the valley interstate,
closed forever without a word.


The fault line rumbles often, a drunken
cyclops. Thick wings of a crow
beat back to a cottonwood bosque.


Nightfall is a blue tide rising.
The moon's silver breaks through
your window. A woman's photo tilts


on the wall above the kitchen table.
She swore to get even. Your raised cup
of Absolut and instant coffee salutes her.

### *Open Tab at Texas Loosey's*

*"To strut yourself where Folly throngs tonight."*
— *Baudelaire*


This joint's all animal heat,
diesel stain
and two-stroke engines.


The barmaid's Latina, leather
chaps, Stetson black as Brynner's
in The Magnificent Seven.


The oval span of the bar top
is her chancel, sanctified
with tabs kept open


by men who laugh hard, as if
to trick her into thinking
they're forlorn of nothing.


I take Shock Top on tap.
Cold foam down the glass
nets her fingers.


She smooths out a towel,
buffs away watermarks
left atop the bar by empties,


recharges my pint.
Doesn't bother to lift to me
those dark eyes of a saint.

## *Evening at the Jenny Rose Restaurant*

Muted light from the 76 station across
the lot falls through the window
onto my plastic blue tablecloth.


A waitress returns from smoke break
in the Mojave night. The cook in back
tunes an aged Motorola to Radio Zion.


The waitress lifts a coffee carafe —
a fissure on its side
like a vein bulged on coke.


The waitress lifts my cup to recharge it,
the restaurant now quiet, near empty.
The light finds its way onto her hands.

## Route 14, North from White Heather

Hell-bent for Bakersfield, wishing tomorrow already
here. On my Chevy's oldies FM, Joan Jett

hates herself for loving some dude. Pondering
her lines, I take a wrong exit, end up

at Love's Travel Stop, just north of Rosamond.
I ask a clerk on smoke break by a pay phone,

about how far I'd yet to go. She had a Marlboro
between fingers wrapped around

a Mountain Dew. She lifted the can,
pointed west, mumbled a number of miles

she thought were too far off, as if to deter me:
someone misdirected by plaintive songs and maps,

the kind of soul who'd post bail for a friend,
knowing damn well he would skip town.

## Classic Ride

All I believe in this hour are 4-barrel carburetors,
a desert mountain's last snow, the deckled
stretch of Mojave roads, their signs that warn:
Pavement Ends; and flash-sightings
of crows and buzzards etching Oro Grande's
sidewalks with shadows.


Or this sleepless night, the stove bulb still on
above cold burners as I watch darkness gather
herself like a cloak above my first floor rooms.


Old engines echo and throb in my hands.
Like the Boss 409 in a friend's '69 Mustang,
before he decided that his classic ride
should challenge a giant mesquite to a duel.


Old talks, older loves lived or un-lived. Mopar
catalogs dog-eared, yearbooks put away.
And some creature treading my roof, glistering
under the streetlight near my garage,
its hide smirched with dust.

## A Little Peace in Yermo
*Mojave Desert, California*


Still near dawn, the upstart sun begins
searing the waterless rivers, greasewood
stands, the windows of our diminutive
post office at the far end of Upton's Market.


Let me explain: life in LA's been out of the question
forever. Out here is a wild that wants nothing
of cities, their seamless mass of suburbs
sewn to a glacial slide of highway traffic.


There's mercy in solitude. Neighbors in need
of nothing more than the air between them.
Though that means our older kids get lonely,
turn fools for meth far away as Bakersfield.


Me, I keep a lean signature — a food-mart
clerk selling discount booze and heat lamp hot dogs
to out-of-towners who could kill us with their eyes
if our ice machine broke down in summer.


On smoke breaks, my boss flicks ashes into his palm,
watches drivers in from Vegas, their wits and wallets
burned from roulette and blackjack. Stopping late
in Yermo, they learn our distance from the world

works hard for its silence as they shake shoulders
of drowsy passengers, uncage their weariness
from cramped cars, hands fumbling for cellphones,
cigarettes, for all they might ever find in the dark.

## *Yucca Valley Song*

Our desert dreams sailed on a flood of reefer
smoke between your mouth and mine.

We've long learned this immersion in distance,
days reduced habitual, like the bonelight

that slips through our curtains, blushing
formica floors, slow-bleaching

plywood that stands-in for a windowpane.
This is the town of overworked motel doors,

shaky deadbolts in stripped wood, sky-tangled
arms of Joshua trees, narrow wildflower

seasons that lure tourists who appear
so briefly — wanderlust sated soon enough.

Yes, we dreamed once: you a park ranger,
me at Ted's Plumbing, happy to live lives

in Goodwill furnishings, a table liberated
from the empty miner's shack

that leaned toward us in Pinto Mountain
winds, our breath stock-still, in fear

of being caught, as if we'd impelled
ourselves to reach home without speaking.

## *Fugitive*

6 a.m., I-10 through Banning Pass. I roll the Peterbilt
window down, let rainy fog chill me awake, fumble
for cigarettes somewhere on the seat.
With dawnlight cresting Indio, I gain a hitchhiker,


maybe 18 or 20. Hair tied back in rubber bands, her eyes
study the road as if she doubts the horizon, or if I might
lose it. We make talk. She says she can't recall
the day she went fugitive from home,


nor said where home was, and I never cared to ask.
I only asked where she was bound. All she replied
was Havasu, and I hate this whole fucking state.
She got out at Flying J truck stop, just past Blythe —


said that was far enough, thanked me, grabbed
my smokes off the dash, and dissolved
into distance and sun-glare. I watch wind sweep
diesel smoke and the reek of rain and reefer


she left in my cab, scents never in a hurry to leave.
Unlike her, time enough to hitchhike to what's needed
in Havasu, from what voices back home
had left her alone with so little time to forgive.

## Travel Music

                    Interstate 15, and my Jeep fights
a brash wind that threads Cajon Pass. The dense
odor of Peterbilt and Mack diesels burn the air.
Satellite radio carries a young voice. She sings
how she is only going over River Jordan.
I'm only going to Barstow, on account I've lost
or forgotten all reasons not to go. It lies yonder,
on the Mojave floor, just beyond Victorville, a town
a friend said years ago was dying. It's certainly
not the yonder of the woman's hymn. Oh Lord,
may my Jordan still be years and untold rivers off.
Praise the verity of gravel, Heaney wrote.
For though railyards, sere riverbeds, crossroads
and café faces like fallen sparrows— all a heart
like mine ever needed—come as numerous
as angels there, Barstow's only Barstow, all the heaven
I seek for now, one more wayfarer who woke
in need of one more town he has never been to.

## *Beyond Bakersfield*

He has signed for the keys to a small house
he now owns a block from Armand's
Diesel Road Service, which tows lame
engines and overheated truckers
off interstates that map the valley.


Scanning the beggared Eden of a backyard,
he takes in the itinerant rage of crows
in the sole camphor tree, the quiet
scent of cottonwoods, and the whisper
of windfall apples decaying into the earth.


Inhaling the pungency of wrought iron
and failed gardens, he turns to gaze across
the street; young daughters of a migrant
farmer pull fistfuls of gold poppies, just
to clutch their brilliance, as their mother


sings a ballad that ascends the midday
heat. Her tune will stay with him like the din
from pry bars and wrenches of Armand's
workers; like the silence of all the women
who said they'd never leave without him.

# This Far North of Mojave

*for Joe Millar*

Eyes tranced and bloodshot from hours on the road,
I pull off Route 101 to overnight in Gilroy. Everything
has found its place here. The odor of harvests grows
sere from drought. Water's reclaimed time and again,

like a weary forgiveness. Main street has shrunk
to antique marts and thrift stores, the tithe of years.
Both coffee shops close on me before I reach their doors.
A bowling alley sign reads 'Good Morning,' no matter

the hour of day. Dogs thrive in the wider reaches
of the town. Reversing my route, I aim for the Chevron
with its food mart. A girl standing beside a blue
Camaro, Texas plates, smokes a bit too close

to the gas pumps. I watch her from the checkout
line, Slim Jims and a Mickey's 40-ounce malt
cold in my fist. Charley Pride, from the cashier's
radio, laments letters he'll never write home.

Now, every shadow retreats. At the Motel 6, I settle
behind double locks in a room around back, walls
stunned with yellow paint. I consider that young lady
back at the Chevron, the soft perfection of her slender

form inhaling tobacco burn like a back-draft, her hair
lifted into sunlight by a ribbon scarlet as regret.
In the all-night distance, the howl of passing trucks
is just far enough off to be a whisper in another room.

## *Cantilena for Barstow*

I'm never sure why I come to these deserts.
Last night in another floundering bar, one
more man called one more woman
a soulless bitch. It sparked a backslap
of flying alcohol that made men look away.


Today a white butterfly fell into my coffee
while a radio voice sang there'll be lightning
in my fists if you're fool enough to show
at my door. I was sufficiently blue inside
to believe it meant the end of grace.


The motel room I took tonight was so quiet
I heard a young couple through walls thin
as the lace she wore for him, while all I have
is the musk of faded wildflowers ghosting
a cracked vase, Venice painted badly on the wall.


The couple's whispers turn to passion. Radio Zion
flutters in static on my nightstand. Spanish
praises God for numbering all the hairs on all
our heads. We creatures strayed from Heaven,
who, at mindless hours, waken and shut our eyes.

# *Reaching Baja from Points North*

I came through winter chaparral wanting
rain that wanted me. It fell on gaunt cattle
in Barrett Junction, on manzanita and shrub
oak, on railroads so endless they seemed
the memory of railroads. It fell on hitchhikers,
their cardboard signs for places I'd never name home.

The storm rumbled against foothills, thick floods
that runneled switchbacks. It reached Tecate
with me, washed the town like a backed-up
dam, the night air swimming with reefer.

I ducked inside Bar Diana, lingered
till a bouncer sent my derelict ass down the street,
wet and cold as a freak blizzard. In the gray
light, I found an inn. The clerk's glare
stung me red when my sodden boots soaked
the lobby carpet, my tongue fumbling foreign.

In a first floor room, thick with ancient
smoke, I shed wet clothes, poured mezcal
I'd bargained at the border, happy for its mock
warmth. I have no reputation to lose,
none to hide, all loose ends intact.

Two American kids quit Diana's
just behind me. They kicked a mongrel
mutt to beat me to this inn. Who knows
what loose ends they'd loosened
wide — a controlled bleed, their love-making
gone animal in the room above my silence.

### House at the Corner of Live Oak and Wheeler Canyon

I was damned glad the law threw those squatters
out of the house some schizoid owner finally quit.
Cleanup commenced in a hustle. Our foreman,
Old Smokey Red, threw a tarp in the bed
of her Ranchero to cart off busted chairs, half a ton
of expired Twinkies, pizza boxes, underthings,
a couch bent and stained with what—no one wants
to know, she and hubby Fernando taking it all
to the city dump. Or so they claimed.


When the time came, Red returned with her lifetime
of yard sale tools, a few no one doubts were pilfered
from neighbors and the plumber across her street.
But don't dare accuse Red of anything unsaintly,
especially with her bolt cutter in one fist, a ripsaw
in the other. And don't dare mock the lunch she'll eat
later of chicken fried steak and Chevron coffee.


Inside, I brush away ads strewn over ancient formica
that shout Everything Must Go at a Sam Levitz shuttered
two years past. I put my crowbar to wood rot
as we get to work, me and three other unlicensed guys
and one of their sons, our hammers, pliers, nails
and plywood doing all they ever do, a dissonant
drumming that rose all day through the neighborhood.

With everything leaning into late day shadows,
we quit for the day. Once this job's done we'll be heroes
to the realtor in her curry-colored trademark jacket.
Red pauses, looks up, blows Pall Mall smoke
moonward, says Don't this damned place just cry out
for mercy, her boot propped on tomorrow's pile
of pale sheetrock, stacked up like pressed flowers.

## *Collector Car Auction, San Bernardino County*

Touting free cocktails the American Legion
would hand out at the hotrod auction, he lured
her to the desert beyond Barstow in his search
for a '60s LeMans, GTO specs. That morning
on the drive from LA, he spoke little, tilted
a smile her way every few miles over
the lumbering grace of open desert. She knew
he wanted that car on the sly, to cut an off-block
deal with a shill. Out her window, her eyes
follow the contours of a vanished river
into the yawning emptiness of the looming Mojave.


On the auction grounds, she waits for him
in the smoking area. Dead tobacco laces the air
around her. She's losing patience, tips her ashes
between pages of the Hemmings Motor News
he asked her to hold. After mindless eons,
he finally drifts her way. His eyes won't telegraph
how the deal went down, but she hopes it went
south as hell. The last thing she wants is some
heap in her Malibu driveway – doesn't give two
shits he's a true believer. Her real frisson
would be the car editing her into its image,
its rebuilt plague of low-brow loudness, her man
gleaming in glandular pride and stink,
grease-monkey groupies sure to flock his glittery,
resurrected junk, all of it endured just to grant
the wish that her own story did not end alone.

## Where Light Widens Beyond Salinas River Inlet

I run derelict from debt and duty for wildflowers
that line the slumbering coast. At Moss Landing,
sun warms the dampness above Elkhorn Slough,
and the sea-battered skiffs someone
never around promises forever to rebuild.


At the world's inland edge, the sun shears in flaxen
light behind a verdant wraith of live oak trees.
My GTO, that rusts in fellowship of sea
and sore bones, exits away from the toil of coastal
traffic shredding the air over Highway 1.


Gulls on the periphery widen their laments. Staves
of a vanished pier rot in languid surf. Along
worn out ribbons of tired slipways, crumbling hulls
console their own decay. Somewhere close
is the soundless threading of campfire smoke into sky.


I divert down a side road into an unpaved lot,
pull up beside an old man in his ancient Ford.
He stares from the cab at plovers breaching
the landward fog beyond us, a few unheard syllables
of his moving lips printing the motionless air.

# *Walking Inland from the Gale*

The storms beyond Catalina Island
darken coastward, as six slim pelicans

slide their inline formation bare inches
atop spindrift, as if beneath radar.

Raindrops pool in a dissonant drumming
on the lid of my paper coffee cup.

Tilting it to my mouth, the rain touches
my lips, cools the already lukewarm drink.

At my lover's house, I'll dry my jacket,
let the rain be evidence I belong.

## Anthem for Pacific Avenue

         San Pedro, that ache
I have for you. For the grace
of common things, the ambient
hum of your midsummer streets,
no sound or scent precise.
I need the alchemy of your two-man
auto shops, burger joints, thrift
stores and taco stands, small
islands of bars—liquor stores
their depots. Even the rescue
mission shouldering its way
between two shuttered storefronts,
a payphone ringing outside,
and no one picking up.

         Maybe that Volvo I need
as well, screeching west,
crammed with possessions, rusty
microwave blocking its back
window, The Righteous Brothers
blaring from the cab. And yes,
even the toppled Kamchatka,
bleeding vodka through bench
boards, a man slouching there,
begging change, a relieved sigh
slipping from his breath
when my coins touch his palm,
as if he had finally been left
in want of nothing.

## San Pedro Harbor, Where the Music Lay

I stared into gray morning light
through a tear in the bedroom curtain,

heard our housekeeper down the hall
on the phone, praying in Spanish

with her sister in Santa Clarita.
It was a day I'd wandered down

to San Pedro harbor. At the pier, I shared
an outdoor patio with Mexican families,

its deck of railroad ties, metal tables,
pigeons ragged from the poverty of scraps,

and a clear view of the fallen countenance
of Terminal Island with its blue-gray

Colby Cranes and shuttered shipyards
bleeding rust from every ancient hinge.

A tugboat named Alta June ushered a barge
without a name, the hunger of commerce.

In the upper air, the Goodyear blimp
was a set-piece in the faultless LA blue.

The Mariachi band that always plays
on the pier drifted near my table, music

I caught but a few words of, as their ballads
echoed over the shipping channel behind me.

## *Harbor Town Soliloquy*

He releases his weight on a wicker bench
set under eaves his house shares

with sparrow nests. Drought abides
like unbroken sleep, town and harbor

sere acolytes of the sun. In a tremolo
of wind, he swirls softly, in mid-summer

heat, a blood-dark sloe gin on the rocks,
jukebox smooth, sipped before a parching

breeze can leave a dust devil in his mouth.
The hills of the peninsula rise in the distance,

sluiced by phosphor wings of gulls. He hails
their passing with a raised glass of sunstruck ice.

## Early March. Harbor Town of San Pedro

I step outside American Tire,
where I've been mounting and balancing
all morning. I light up a Winston, lie to myself
that I've been cutting back. Giant blue anvils
of nimbus storms hang heavy over the coast,
over strike-torn shipping lanes of LA harbor,
its container ships hulking in silent, wakeless water.

My work day done by 3:00, I trudge exhausted
a few short blocks to the seafront. Wind
tinged with diesel and salt rises and falls over
languid fishing boats that pull at hawsers leashing
them to land. Sky dense with shorebird song
echoes through empty rooms behind vanished
panes of shuttered canneries just across the channel.

A gray light slants over fish markets where the poor
take what they can from the sea. I take a wobbly
table at Boardwalk Café. Alejandra brings beer
and a frown. She knows I'll tip lousy, my paycheck
halved by alimony and other mortal habits.
Now and then, crows settle on empty tables, rifle
castoff paper plates and cups like noisy thieves.

I know I could be anyone alive here. Sipping a third
Modelo. Pondering a rat that scrambles over the pier
suspended above the channel, hungering toward
the dense odor of a rotting gull, or the breeze
coming ashore from goods stagnating on the container
ship. Mere feet below, a starfish, its arms a bright
compass rose, lies unmoving in the shallows.

## Fiesta Cruise Day, San Pedro Harbor

Men and stone are ancient where cities touch
the sea. Hawsers creak in berths, and forklifts

cut the light. Blades of choppers beat
the autumn air. Giant tournefortia shade

private docks. I amble boardwalks, seafood
stands, watch the harbor waken, crabs fresh

off boats — shocked by sudden cold
of clear and foreign water. Engines thrum

like hangovers, pull ships astern
through the wake of Alta June, a tug

that owns the sea lane. Across the channel,
the Bethlehem plant that sent destroyers

to the last good war, sits a monument to rust
under Colby Cranes, there since '43. The Goodyear

blimp, a pastel ash in the chalk-blue distance,
floats in descent through brassy midday light.

The carousel, there forever, has been hauled
away, its florid horses rumored mean by children.

### San Pedro January

*for David Goodis*


Winter never ices this port city,
but stays offshore in steel-blue
Caravaggio clouds, in sub-zeroes
that never reach us.


First time I took 6th Street
up from the docks, windfall hulls
of magnolia leaves rattled
like castanets from an unseen zambra.


I found myself in the Indian Room bar,
its dun hollow framed against an open
doorway, a place Icarus might've come
to drown the tremble of his wings,


had he survived. Like me, he could've
watched a breeze gust the pages
of a castoff horoscope, as if no one
inside were allowed the amnesty of fortune.

## *Two Urchin Divers at Terminal Island*

I've long heard how the men reap
starburst thorns from outer bay
floors, docking their catch on shaky
wooden piers, dreaming at length

of grand hauls, making their late
afternoon way to meld among us
at Harbor Light for beer, as waves
furl against the bow of their boat,

its rainbow of oil clouding the stern.
Between drinks, I heard one recall
his father, who left this harbor one
Monday in summer, outbound without

a misgiving, his suitcase in the boat's
hold, shoeless in cutoffs and tee-shirt,
how he resurfaced years later. I listened
a bit longer, stood and turned for home,

relieving them of my trespass. A salt
wind brushed past me in the doorway
from whatever compass it followed
that day, passing through armadas

of container ships, through scaffolds
of cranes flooding the horizon,
through our steps—casual or hurried—
through our unrelenting island.

## Terminal Island, Los Angeles Harbor

*"In the dark you can love this place."*
*Philip Levine, "Scouting"*

The fish plant I work at fills the emptiness
at the end of a pier, out where tugboats shove
the dull names of barges beyond Angels Gate
lighthouse, on into Pacific starlight.

Our job titles sound so terse and primitive
you'd think they were dreamed up by Adam
on the beleaguered road out of Eden:
Sorter, Trimmer, Peeler, Dumper.

I join the swing shift late, enter once
more the processing room I've worked in
half a year now, slide into protective
gloves and apron while the boss lady

calls out commands to goldbricks,
like Fernando and Bob racing handtrucks
as I take my paring knife to core mackerel
passed down from the sorting tables.

My boss is a quiet one – worked here forever,
her eyes a vigil for slowdowns and jam-ups
on slicing machines and conveyers. Tonight
she grabs her smokes to go on break with me.

We pass others taking in the ocean air, the surf
close and black as we round the corner
for Harbor Lights and its stiff coffee, to know
again the rusty aftertaste as we'll stare out

from our booth at the darkened casements
of shipyards, their generators long fallen
silent; the faded copper glow of streetlamps,
like faces, pushing softly against our window.

## Shipyard Sonata

He surveys the barges moving out in early
dark from harbors that bring the sea
    to the shore-bound world. They glide out past
    docklands, the breakwater lighthouse; the amber


glow of berth and pier a soft drowse over
the nightfall waters, the Pacific surf
    undulant with the swing of constellations
    as women stare seaward from high windows.


In the doorway of the sheetmetal shop,
he hears the faint pulse of outbound
    commerce and is pained with a longing
    he'll quickly dismiss. He bolts the door behind him,


turns toward home, leaving alone for this one night
the men of sea and harbor who quench thirst
    under a warm array of strung neon, spending
    all the mercy that won't save itself for tomorrow.

## Variation on the Neighbor Across the Street

Streetlight falls in a pale aura around the Ranchero
she reclines in the bed of, her head slightly back,
a broken couch hauled off from somewhere
boosting her in its musty grip, her blue-jeaned thighs

spread in defiance of all etiquette save solitude—
near graceless, a patron at a Left Bank café,
her eyes dark as Delvaux's nightfall women.
Long exhales from a long brand of cigarettes

are a private sacrament that puts a haze between her
and the clarity of this cloudless night, where galaxies
bleed faint silver through the California sky.
I watch, for an hour plus, as she gazes upward

as if seeking some tender or fragile mystery
in the mindless distance above, the breath-flamed
tip of a fresh cigarette a semaphore in the dark
beyond my living room window. I think

of her mind's eye tracing some unseen star-fall
over fissures, like scars, in the streets she'll drive
before dawn, her blown smoke gliding densely,
its gray pall a harbinger through the gaining fog.

## Stopping at Texas Looseys on a Warm Monday Homeward

Don't judge the man for the sheer
digressions that specter through him.
No. Judge him for this:


The boilermaker's midday vertigo,
the sweat and backstory of gin,
playing Rare Earth's Get Ready —
the longest number in jukebox history.


\*


The barmaid's a Latina cowgirl,
or someone disguised as one:
black hat, leather chaps,
a waistline low as lust,
and he can't recall whether
she's Jacqueline or Jasmine.


On the bar TV, the Fonz
degrades himself
with a realty commercial.
So much for cool
when you're nothing
but a 1-800 number.


\*

Four stools down, a dude his age,
late '50s, sits with his daughter,
hairy of arm and leg.


He won't bet they'll make
the lingerie show tonight.
Not sure he'll make it either,
stumbling now into the men's room,
his dignity ever more in doubt
as he trips toward a whitewashed
wall that looks like his future
hungering toward him.

## Syllabic Lines for Laundry Hung Dirty on a Friday Afternoon

Today, LA weather has a one-track
mind, wry enough to fake an end to the drought.
Across the street, a woman I've never

met, but call 'Ol Smokey Red, is hauled off
by cops for rabbit-punching her old man.
I stare at a ladder that leans against

her house. It has never been taken down.
No one has ever climbed its vacant rungs
that ascend above the plane of the roof.

Down a flanking street, in a house of five
daughters, what has gone wrong goes wrong again
in harsh voices that shake the idle leaves

of my camphor tree. Empty glass in hand
I step through my doorway, a spider web's
invisible silk just brushing my lips.

## *Taking on the Record LA Heat*

By high-noon the sun was a withering fire
on the I-110 South to San Pedro. Sweat

and industrial harbor air stung my face.
I'd gone for a cold Pabst at the Indian

Room on Pacific. Three old whiskey angels
were the end of the bar. I let them drink

alone. I took a barstool beside a man
who said Pabst is from his hometown

of La Crosse, at the confluence of the Indian
and Black Rivers where they dog-leg down

to the Mississippi. He's a Vietnam vet,
but says no one cares in Bumfuck, Wyoming,

though I'm not sure how he got there from here.
I simply replied with a line from Burroughs—

Some habits take your gut on the way out.
Perhaps our bar talk ran portent this morning:

I'd seen a neighborhood crow flutter up
from its whore-bath in stagnant runoff and leaves.

It perched on a neighbor's gable, its dark
wet feathers a luster in the warming winds.

## The Regular at the Five Star Bar

You're downtown LA,
and a barmaid
you've got twenty years on
if you've got a day,
high-fives you for playing
Roger Miller's "In the Summertime"
on the juke. As if that ancient
tune from a late singer
who'd served in the Korean
War to avoid jail for stealing
a guitar was somehow
the ballad of her own youth.


In the visceral slap of her palm
your faith is renewed
that the best music never dies,
abides by its own
calendar in backstreet
hovels like these. When you rise
from a piece of mismatched
furniture to leave, the music
inhabits you with all the surety
of the shadow you'll cast
on the 3rd Street sidewalk,
that dark outline indelible
ink that owns you.

### Subdividing Heaven and Earth in
### Downtown LA

*"Nothing dies as slowly as a scene."*
— *Richard Hugo*


City of Angels hard-pressed to be found beyond
the barmaids in the Five Star on Spring and 3rd.
City of women who smell good double-timing


past me on warm November sidewalks. City
panhandling for bus fare that burns holes in pockets
already burned-through. Of foot traffic whose eyes


wear the Dodgers' final playoff loss. City of glass
and steel progress that scythes the sleep of the sleepless
recessed in sealed doorways. Noir city where ghosts


in the Palace Theater rattle the exit doors. City
that won't bother to squelch its five-alarm lust
and never asks forgiveness for angels thrown


to concrete like lightning from Heaven. City of Angels
that fall more than rise. Sun that won't quit
laying its late-day shadows on my back – shadows


that glide like ships down Gallery Row, daylight
in this city without a winter, of Solo Deo Gloria
over a soup kitchen window. City of sky

bluing the same shade as the eyes of a woman
in a chiffon shawl, swinging her hips and shielding
her vision from the light that divides the empty windows

of St. George hotel, sifts trees in Pershing Square.
City of heads bowed in the backdraft of fire trucks
shooting in exigence down South Main. City

where in a green room in the Southpark Hotel
I'll lie sleepless and wait for the moon to wax
or wane on the cold bedroom walls.

## After Losing the Plea Bargain

In the sleepless dark of the St. George
Hotel, in this City of uneasy Angels,

he drew his watch absurdly close
to his face, hoping the dial caught

enough ambient light from earlier
hours to make a legible glow. He lit

a Lucky Strike, let the match flame bend
to his extinguishing breath. Sliding back

the curtain, he glanced up at the moon
caught like Absalom in the canopy

of camphor trees. On the edge
of its sickle, he hung his bitterness.

## When the Triggering Towns are Never Far Away

Only because it was on my way between
somewhere and elsewhere, I stopped
at Chateau Liquor for some kind of diet
soda, or maybe a lumpy green swill
all the machine-stamped blondes in LA
gulp down. In front of me in line
was a middle-aged, burnt-out surfer fop,
his face shriveled as an endless summer.
He tells the clerk, "The doc told me to lay off
the hard stuff, so I traded Three Olives Vodka
for Old English 800 – something with a polite
name." His girlfriend or date or otherwise
squeeze-of-day says, "You still gonna wake up
heartbroke and hung-over, baby." "What the hell
ya want me to do," he replies, "buy one of those
fake barley-water beers?" In her weirdly huge
right fist were three cans of Busch –
which I didn't think they still made,
and which caused me a moment's flashback
to a purple '74 Duster. She cocked her head,
raised the beers, and said, "Try this instead!
This shit'll go easier on ya!" They checked
out, sauntered to the corner of Anza
and Sepulveda to hitchhike under an LA sky
as blue as a drought, bragging how they'll catch
a lift to Bakersfield before sundown, a few drinks
with strangers, repeating their stories at any cost.

## Halfway House, Downtown Los Angeles

By the time he booked into St. George's Hotel,
Room 204 — across from Wild-Ass Willie

and a kid who'd burned his liver out at twenty-four —
the keys he'd saved from doors he lived behind

totaled fourteen. He kept them on a necklace his girlfriend
gave back before splitting for Denver for good.

We, his fellow addicts-in-overhaul, hear his derelict
breathing behind the door he never locks,

muttering the way our last counselor did.
She left us cold after a bandwagon fall of her own.

Her replacement swore she never liked it here anyway
— none of us losers, damned pleased to find a home

in another city, driving alone all night to get there.

## Seven Men Break Silence at a Union Rescue Mission Meal

Sun-gristled, they glide in silhouette past our kitchen
door, their undertones low enough, a music without origin...

One fall, our lab run off. From an upper window, dad
swore at me. Said it was 'cause I named him wrong.

I climbed the avenue to get here late yesterday.
Got left outside like a dog's water bowl.

My atheist daughter climbed Mt. Lemmon
to be closer to her dead brother.

A woman told me laughing's just another way
to kiss. Left my laugh under the ice in her glass.

I come by yesterday. They was closed. I leaned
against this door. Swear I heard jokin' inside.

Done tried my hand at a love poem. But the eclipse
slurred my moonbeam in a soft-focus lens.

Got here late. Saw light under the door. Slept right
there. Soft as a child carried to sleep up a flight of stairs.

## *Union Station Landscaper*
*Los Angeles*


Sanders too I was blessed to have known,
his realm the plots of overgrowth and failing
flowers on Alameda Street, the 101 off-ramp


his truck screams down late each morning, arms
full of rakes and trowels in textbook labor,
resolute in his stint but far from flawless, his eyes


numbering the homeless strewn like effigies
along the station's grass, coffee shaking in his fist
from a thermos cracked from falling out


of the truck bed, lunch breaks with malt bottles
and deli meat on black rye, day's end the grime
and glory of an aching body he takes home


over the 1st Street Bridge, tossing bottles
into the LA River, browning below, where castoff
blossoms always find their way to the sea.

### The Week after Mass at Saint Alphonsus, East LA

Padre Fernando preached that every good and perfect
gift comes down from the Father of Lights.


My own gift was the warm smile of a truckstop waitress
who came to me by way of a bad divorce in Hermosillo.


After we agreed with padre to make a truce with lust,
she and I escaped for a week to Baja – coastal Ensenada.


So we only held hands, like grade school kids, but allowed
warm kisses between cool sips of Sol Brava malt.


In the mornings we'd walk the beach, watch the tide
go out, speak of the good padre back home on Amalia


Avenue, wonder aloud how parishioners always taxed
his patience, and all he knows of how much we need


forgiveness, as we gripped the warm salt of each other's
hands; the broken, luminous seashells cutting our feet.

## LA Redux on an Ancient Parable

I waited for the courthouse to open
this morning, a misdemeanor charge
of loitering hung over my head.


A woman in line behind me told someone
on her phone, "My prodigal son's
dragged his ass back to the swine trough."


At midday, fine paid, I watch a scrap
metal truck pass, its bed full. Castoff
iron and steel glinting, like scars of light.

## Days Beyond the Wager

Hollywood Park is not your exit now.
Quitting tote boards that sealed your hours to luck

only means you can't forgive the losers –
neither jockeys thrown nor stumbling horses

that burned your bets on Sunday afternoons,
days now gone as big-timer, sweeping cards.

That blue-eyed girl at the bar would always
absolve you of doubts. She killed time for you

like a promise stretched miles beyond repair,
you shipwrecked Odysseus of shit luck.

So swear your hope is in that woman's wine,
and hedge bets she couldn't jinx with a kiss.

## Redondo Beach Notebook

Summer morning, sugared alchemies of choice
swirl in bright cafe cups, patrons rousing
from the undertow of rising August

heat. Speech unfolds in greetings breathed
half inside hot liquids brought to lips
that greet the day in whispers, kisses, curses.

I find the homeless guy, one who never quits
talking long enough to ask his name, in prone sleep
on the grassy square in front of Wells Fargo,

mere feet from its door. He seems an exhausted
messenger, or one shot despite the proverb,
a breeze pulling at his shirt, his head full of words

silenced for once, a dream's backroom voice—
calling him by that name I've never learned,
still wondering how his story ever ended.

## *Artesia Boulevard Story*

*Redondo Beach, California*


Somewhere between the claw hammer
I bought on sale from Kurt's True Value
and the Shell station coffee and 7-11
hot wings now burning my gut, this cool
November morning ascends the bric-a-brac
mothball and tobacco air of the Goodwill
I exit, a stuffed Santa slumping like a drunk
in the corner of its storefront window.
I pass Mexican landscapers taking their break
of Gatorade and tacos in the shade
of Pep Boys auto. A drunk on a bus stop
bench wants to show me in his slurred
lexicon a card trick he calls three card monte.


But I pass his offer up, hope against hope
the door of Bac Street Lounge is unlocked,
its marquee wishing someone named
Ashley a Happy Birthday. But luck won't answer
my tug at the door, resistance saying come back
later, this street I may or may not return
to after dark, its neon like mascara bleeding over
sidewalks under the cold rind of the waning
moon, the last clerk, locking up Goodwill,
blowing a tired cloud of smoke that rides
her breath like sparrows through the dark.

## *Pacing Inland from Redondo Beach*
## *in Winter*

At the shoreline, I turn from thin rainbows
that flash in the spindrift of light-struck breakers,
head homeward to the house my woman
and I share. She'd split with another man a short
while back on account he'd come home to her
with the reek of late-night strippers.


Coming up on Vista del Mar Apartments, a new
occupant's replaced the blight of gaunt blue
curtains I thought would be up forever, with a rebirth
of green. At a first floor window though, a cheerless
white drape remains canted, as if a shut-in's
furtive eye tracked strangers on the street.


Along the storefront of Inge's Fashions,
the blue-haired owner outfits manikins in gold
and glitter, slides outsized sunglasses on
and slips out the back to light a Marlboro,
puffs a gray cloud through heavy red lipstick
as my hand shields the glare of the winter sun.


In due course I reach the lettered avenues, rooftops
with antennas that wait-out corrosive time
for signals that will never return. At one house
with immaculate lawn and spotless driveway, twin
valentines gild the front door. They beam side-by-side,
a scarlet symmetry of kisses printing the light.

# *Inheriting the Earth on Avenue F*

The squinting eyes of wanderers on the streets
look like creases in maps, or just decades of harsh
news as they pass bars that hold all the regressive
darkness of Hopper's rooms – Pat's Place
where the barmaid will ask if house whiskey
is okay or do you want something better, just
a couple hours after you've shared a coffee
with those wanderers this early Thursday,
finding you love most their sadness, the slipping
in and out of the world, each time returning
a little less of themselves, regulars who must get
their Marlboros or Kools at Fernando's Liquor
where the aged owner rubs the well-earned
pain screaming in his shoulder, one more pained
alleluia of survival, the Palos Verdes hills ascending
through filaments of soft gray light, the wind
in its cold purity driving sea fog shoreward,
the labor of high contrails passing overhead –
always someone going home, and your new love
who tells you each day that you are her very
heart, is on your front steps now, shielding
her eyes against the wild morning light.

### Thursday at the Torrance Salvation Army Thrift Shop

Coffee mugs from garish resorts, or towns
you've never heard of, and cups that boast
the world's greatest mother or grandfather.

Fabric flowers are stacked next to a stand
of neckties even Bozo wouldn't dare, arrayed
beneath prints from vanished hotel rooms.

A poster for televisions says "TV tested good" –
as if it was first put on sale for moral problems.
But a sign above says the antenna's not for sale.

Dirty crockpots line up like soup kitchen men
who might hold for mere water the glasses
etched in Taiwan with obsolete superheroes.

A black guitar case leans against another.
They could've hitchhiked in from somewhere,
finally grown tired of their own music.

As I survey the shop one last time, a woman
asks if she can leave by the back exit,
a Drew Barrymore movie poster in her arms.

People departing the shop touch piano keys
as they pass the Steger & Sons grand.
They're always those who could never play.

## West Long Beach Littoral for Late April

There's a hotel without a name near Miramar
and Anaheim, where occupants drop
what possessions they own on dusty mattresses.
You didn't dwell long on whatever loss
brought you there, locked the door behind
you, and hit the twilight streets under a weak
moon rising in the soft impeachment of early
evening. At Rudy's Diner, you waited for a warm
meal dowsed in Tabasco, the heady acid
jolting a cough, a bite of hash browns chased
with bitter coffee. Bill paid, you passed a woman
at the entryway phone begging someone
in Spanish to please come home. Avoiding her eyes,
you paced west on Anaheim, stopped at Rosita's
Flowers, blossoms locked behind a thrown bolt.
Above, night birds fluttered from a window ledge
into wind rising shoreward that smelled of iron
and the sea. Reversing steps, you came to the railyard
at Cerritos Channel and paused, wondered
if there was more out there, knowing the answer
was a search for nothing promised, all thought
haloed under liquor store neon – an arrow aimed
inward like a one-way sign, nightfall bringing
all the sirens ever needed to sing your way home.

# Triptych for Terminal Island Docks

I.


The way the late sun arcs through a window at Harbor Light
Café to brighten a page from Bukowski or Levine might gather
the trades of beleaguered workers the way they appear
in want ads — machinist, welder, cook, driver — ads
begrudged and curt: we'll hire if we absolutely must.


II.


The café reader will have his fries and catfish,
eat with the indifferent gaze of the sea. He'll stuff the book
into a thigh pocket, feel the poet's lines press against his leg.
They insist laments into every task, every tuna bin he hauls
ashore, every forklift he mounts, each joint and muscle
falling behind his body's stiff schedule.


III.


Let the tuna, worn trawlers, and sea lions that ease themselves
onto abandoned pilings feel the light unfold around them,
sorting each from giant shadows of cranes and container ships.
Let everything take its chances here through the light
that rides the harbor, the vague fortunes of berths and slips,
the reborn barge at Larson's boat repair, released to tunes
of milling machines and drill presses as it backs its way seaward,
the dead tired soul who stumbles through his shift on burnt
coffee and luck, all those laments that would catch him as he falls.

**Jeffrey Alfier's** collection of Southwest poems, *Idyll for a Vanishing River* (Glass Lyre Press), won the 2014 Kithara Book Prize. His latest chapbooks are *Bleak Music*, a photograph and poetry collaboration with Larry D. Thomas (Blue Horse Press, 2016), *Southbound Express to Bay Head — New Jersey Poems* (Grayson Books, 2016) and *The Red Stag at Carrbridge — Scotland Poems* (Aldrich, 2016). *Anthem for Pacific Avenue*, a collection of California poems, is due out in 2017. Recent credits include Cold Mountain Review, Southern Poetry Review and Hotel Amerika. He is founder and co-editor of Blue Horse Press and *San Pedro River Review*.